JULIUS · S · HELD
RUBENS DRAWINGS
PHAIDON

MCMLIX

A LIONESS. London, British Museum

RUBENS

SELECTED DRAWINGS

WITH AN INTRODUCTION
AND A CRITICAL CATALOGUE
BY JULIUS · S · HELD

VOL · II

THE PLATES

PHAIDON PRESS · LONDON

CONTENTS

THE PLATES

I : SKETCHES FOR COMPOSITIONS
(PLATES 1–79)

II : STUDIES FROM MODELS AND PORTRAITS
(PLATES 80–139)

III : LANDSCAPES
(PLATES 140–147)

IV : DESIGNS FOR SCULPTURES, ENGRAVINGS AND WOODCUTS
(PLATES 148–164)

V : COPIES BY RUBENS AFTER OTHER MASTERS AND DRAWINGS RETOUCHED BY RUBENS
(PLATES 165–179)

LIST OF PLATES

LIST OF COLLECTIONS

THE PLATES

I
SKETCHES FOR COMPOSITIONS

1 (Cat. No. 1) THE DISCOVERY OF CALLISTO. Berlin, Kupferstichkabinett

2 (Cat. No. 2) A BATTLE OF GREEKS AND AMAZONS. London, British Museum

3 (Cat. No. 5) CHRIST CROWNED WITH THORNS. Brunswick, Herzog Anton Ulrich-Museum

4 (Cat. No. 3) THE DESCENT FROM THE CROSS. Leningrad, Hermitage

5 (Cat. No. 4) THE ENTOMBMENT OF CHRIST. Rotterdam, Museum Boymans

6 (Cat. No. 6) THE RETURN OF THE VICTORIOUS HORATIUS. New York, Metropolitan Museum of Art

7 (Cat. No. 7) SKETCHES FOR THE LAST SUPPER. Chatsworth, Devonshire Collection

8 (Cat. No. 7 verso) MEDEA AND HER SLAIN CHILDREN. Reverse of Plate 7. Chatsworth, Devonshire Collection

10 (Cat. No. 9) THISBE COMMITTING SUICIDE.
Brunswick (Maine), Collection of Mrs. Stanley P. Chase

9 (Cat. No. 8) STUDIES FOR THE SUICIDE OF THISBE.
Paris, Louvre

11 (Cat. No. 12) THE BIRTH OF THE VIRGIN. Paris, Petit Palais

12 (Cat. No. 11) THE BAPTISM OF CHRIST. Paris, Louvre

13 (Cat. No. 13) THE DEATH OF CREUSA. Bayonne, Musée Bonnat

14 (Cat. No. 14) THE BATTLE OF LAPITHS AND CENTAURS. Amsterdam, Rijksmuseum

15 (Cat. No. 10) CAIN SLAYING ABEL. Amsterdam, Fodor Collection

16 (Cat. No. 15) JUDITH KILLING HOLOFERNES. Frankfurt, Städelsches Kunstinstitut

17 (Cat. No. 20) SUSANNA. Montpellier, Bibliothèque Universitaire

18 (Cat. No. 16) ST. GREGORY, ST. MAURUS AND ST. PAPIANUS.
Chantilly, Musée Condé

19 (Cat. No. 17) THE IMAGE OF THE VIRGIN ADORED BY ANGELS. Vienna, Albertina

20 (Cat. No. 18) TWO SHEPHERDS AND MAN WITH TURBAN.
Amsterdam, Fodor Collection

21 (Cat. No. 24) SAMSON AND DELILA. Amsterdam, Collection of J.Q. van Regteren Altena

22 (Cat. No. 23) VENUS LAMENTING ADONIS. London, Collection of Ludwig Burchard

23 (Cat. No. 22) VENUS LAMENTING ADONIS. London, British Museum

24 (Cat. No. 21) THE DEATH OF HIPPOLYTUS. Bayonne, Musée Bonnat

26 (Cat. No. 30) TWO STUDIES FOR ST. CHRISTOPHER.
London, British Museum

25 (Cat. No. 19) A BACCHANAL.
Antwerp, Cabinet des Estampes

28 (Cat. No. 26) DAVID AND GOLIATH. Montpellier, Bibliothèque Universitaire

27 (Cat. No. 25) DAVID AND GOLIATH. Rotterdam, Museum Boymans

29 (Cat. No. 31) THE CONVERSION OF ST. PAUL. London, Collection of Count Antoine Seilern

30 (Cat. No. 29) SILENUS AND AEGLE, AND OTHER FIGURES. Windsor Castle, Royal Library

31 (Cat. No. 32) BATHSHEBA RECEIVING DAVID'S LETTER. Berlin, Kupferstichkabinett

32 (Cat. No. 34) HERCULES STRANGLING THE NEMEAN LION. Antwerp, Cabinet des Estampes

33 (Cat. No. 27) STUDIES FOR THE VISITATION. Bayonne, Musée Bonnat

34 (Cat. No. 28) STUDIES FOR THE PRESENTATION IN THE TEMPLE.
New York, Metropolitan Museum of Art

35 (Cat. No. 37) THE ENTOMBMENT OF CHRIST. Amsterdam, Rijksmuseum

36 (Cat. No. 33) TWO STUDIES OF A RIVER-GOD. Boston, Museum of Fine Arts

37 (Cat. No. 36) THREE ROBED MEN. Copenhagen, Kunstmuseet

38 (Cat. No. 35) THE ASSUMPTION OF THE VIRGIN. Vienna, Albertina

39 (Cat. No. 42) THE DESCENT FROM THE CROSS. Collection of the late Mrs. G. W. Wrangham

40 (Cat. No. 38) THE CONTINENCE OF SCIPIO. Berlin, Kupferstichkabinett

41 (Cat. No. 39) THE CONTINENCE OF SCIPIO. Bayonne, Musée Bonnat

42 (Cat. No. 41) STUDIES FOR A DRUNKEN SILENUS. Collection of the late Mrs. G. W. Wrangham

43 (Cat. No. 43) THE RAISING OF LAZARUS. Berlin, Kupferstichkabinett

44 (Cat. No. 40) THE APOSTLES SURROUNDING THE VIRGIN'S TOMB. Oslo, Nasjonalgalleriet

45 (Cat. No. 44) THE LAST COMMUNION OF ST. FRANCIS. Antwerp, Cabinet des Estampes

Above: 46 (Cat. No. 45) FEMALE NUDES RECLINING. London, Collection of Count Antoine Seilern
Below: 47 (Cat. No. 46) STUDIES FOR VENUS AND CUPID. New York, Frick Collection

48 (Cat. No. 48) HERCULES STANDING ON DISCORD, CROWNED BY TWO GENII.
London, British Museum

49 (Cat. No. 47) ST. GREGORY NAZIANZENUS. New York, Collection of Clarence L. Hay

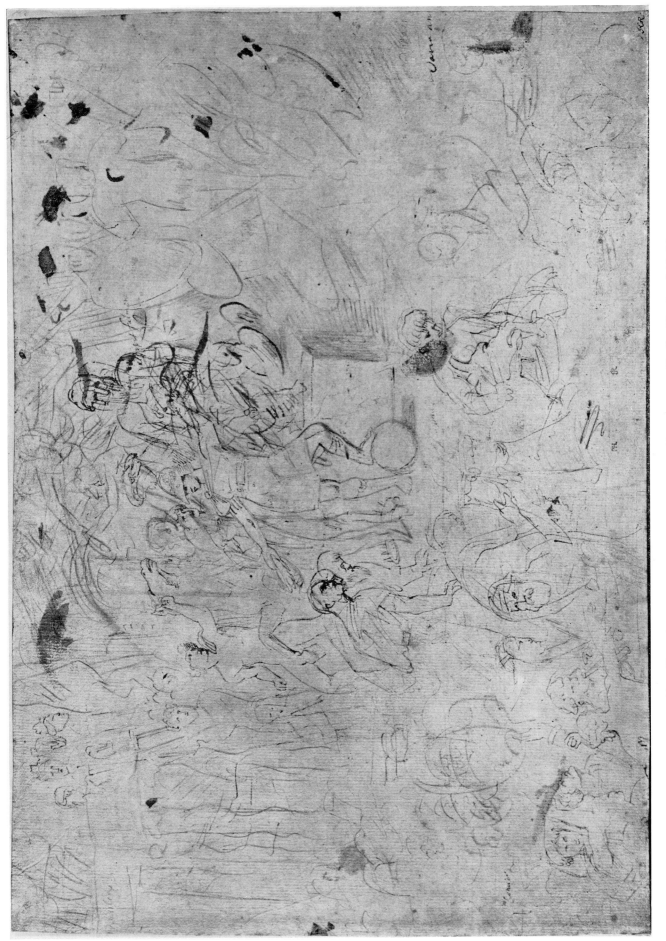

50 (Cat. No. 52) STUDIES FOR A ROMAN TRIUMPH. Berlin, Kupferstichkabinett

51 (Cat. No. 49) ROMA TRIUMPHANS. Vienna, Albertina

52 (Cat. No. 50 recto) THE VESTAL TUCCIA. Paris, Louvre

53 (Cat. No. 50 verso) LOUIS XIII COMES OF AGE. Paris, Louvre

54 (Cat. No. 51 recto) MARIE DE MÉDICIS RECEIVES THE OLIVE BRANCH OF PEACE.
Formerly Bremen, Kunsthalle

55 (Cat. No. 51 verso) HENRY IV CARRIED TO HEAVEN AND OTHER FIGURES. Reverse of Plate 54.
Formerly Bremen, Kunsthalle

56 (Cat. No. 55 recto) FEMALE NUDES RECLINING. London, Collection of Count Antoine Seilern

57 (Cat. No. 55 verso) CENTAURS EMBRACING. Reverse of Plate 56

58 (Cat. No. 53 verso) STUDIES FOR THE VIRGIN AND CHILD; AND STUDIES FOR ST. GEORGE
AND THE DRAGON. Reverse of Plate 59

59 (Cat. No. 53 recto) THE VIRGIN ADORED BY SAINTS. Stockholm, Nationalmuseum

60 (Cat. No. 53 verso) ST. GEORGE AND THE DRAGON. Detail of Plate 58

61 (Cat. No. 54) STUDIES FOR ST. GEORGE AND THE PRINCESS. Berlin, Kupferstichkabinett

62 (Cat. No. 58) VENUS ANADYOMENE AND TWO NEREIDS. London, British Museum

63 (Cat. No. 56) A NYMPH ASLEEP. Rotterdam, Museum Boymans

64 (Cat. No. 62) THE THREE GRACES. London, Collection of Count Antoine Seilern

65 (Cat. No. 59, 60) WOMEN HARVESTING. Edinburgh, National Gallery of Scotland

66 (Cat. No. 59, 60) WOMEN HARVESTING. Edinburgh, National Gallery of Scotland

67 (Cat. No. 57 verso) DANCING PEASANTS. London, British Museum

68 (Cat. No. 57 verso) Detail of Plate 67

69 (Cat. No. 57 verso) Detail of Plate 67

70 (Cat. No. 57 recto) STUDIES FOR A KERMESSE. Reverse of Plate 67. London, British Museum

71 (Cat. No. 57 recto) Detail of Plate 70

72 (Cat. No. 63) THE ADORATION OF THE MAGI. Besançon, Musée des Beaux-Arts

73 (Cat. No. 61) STUDIES FOR THE EXPLOITS OF HERCULES. London, British Museum

74 (Cat. No. 66) HERCULES AND MINERVA FIGHTING MARS. Paris, Louvre

76 (Cat. No. 65 recto) CUPID CAPTURED. Reverse of Plate 75

75 (Cat. No. 65 verso) NYMPH AND SATYR. Berlin, Kupferstichkabinett

77 (Cat. No. 67) THE FEAST OF HEROD. Cleveland, Museum of Art

78 (Cat. No. 64) DIANA AND HER NYMPHS. London, Collection of Count Antoine Seilern

79 (Cat. No. 68) LANDSQUENETS CAROUSING. Paris, Collection of Frits Lugt

II
STUDIES FROM MODELS
AND PORTRAITS

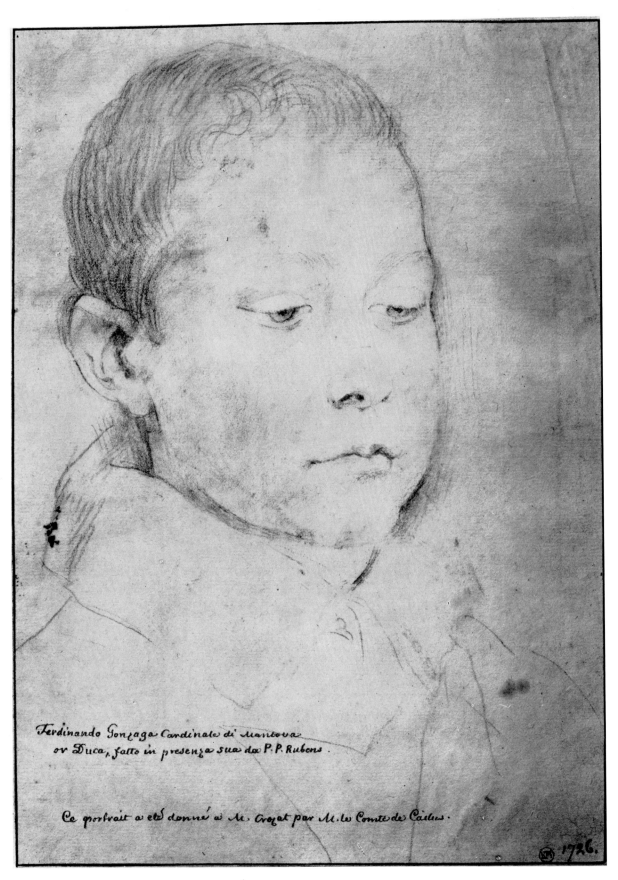

Ferdinando Gonzaga Cardinale di Mantova
ov Duca, fatto in presenza sua da P. P. Rubens.

Ce portrait a été donné a M. Crozat par M. le Comte de Caylus.

1726.

80 (Cat. No. 69) PORTRAIT OF FERDINANDO I GONZAGA, PRINCE OF MANTUA.
Stockholm, Nationalmuseum

81 (Cat. No. 70) MAN HOLDING THE SHAFT OF THE CROSS. Bayonne, Musée Bonnat

82 (Cat. No. 72) YOUNG SOLDIER WITH HALBERD. London, Collection of Michael Jaffé

83 (Cat. No. 71) GENTLEMAN IN ARMOUR ON HORSEBACK. Paris, Louvre

84 (Cat. No. 73) PORTRAIT OF A LADY. London, Collection of Edmund Schilling

85 (Cat. No. 74) ST. CATHERINE. London, Collection of Ludwig Burchard

86 (Cat. No. 78) A FARM GIRL WITH FOLDED HANDS. Rotterdam, Museum Boymans

87 (Cat. No. 76) NUDE MAN WITH RAISED ARMS.
The Hague, Collection of H.R.H. Princess Wilhelmina of the Netherlands

88 (Cat. No. 75) NUDE MAN, KNEELING. Rotterdam, Museum Boymans

89 (Cat. No. 77) STUDIES OF HEADS AND HANDS. Vienna, Albertina

90 (Cat. No. 81) STUDIES OF HEADS AND HANDS. Vienna, Albertina

91 (Cat. No. 80) STUDY FOR JOB. Stockholm, Nationalmuseum

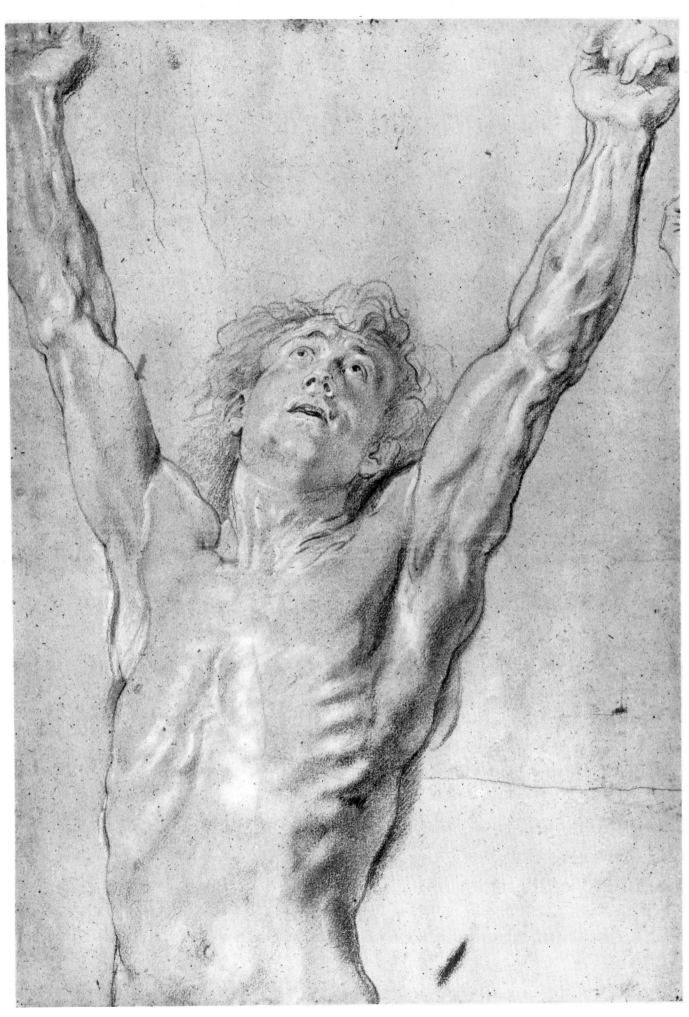

92 (Cat. No. 82) STUDY FOR THE FIGURE OF CHRIST ON THE CROSS. London, British Museum

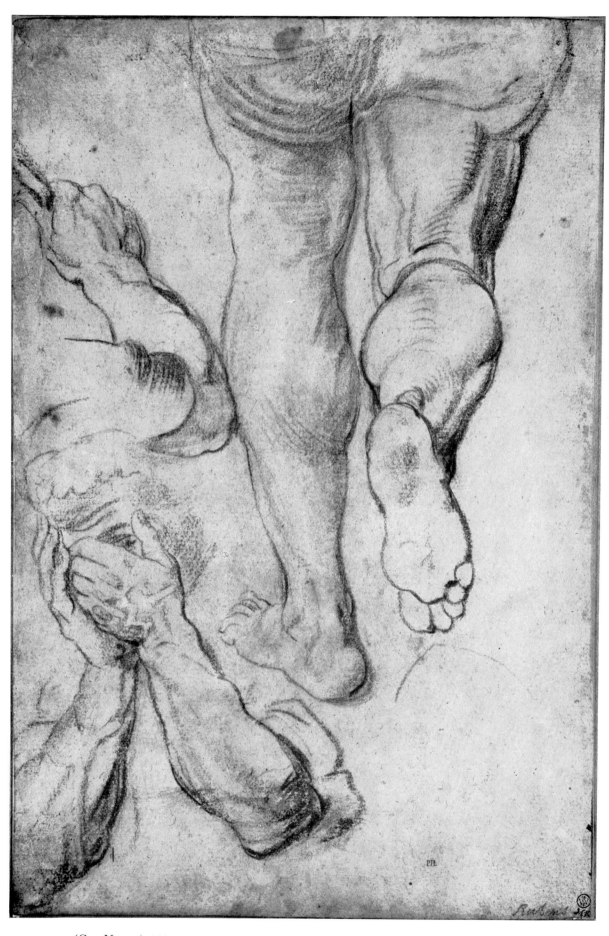

93 (Cat. No. 79) STUDIES OF ARMS AND LEGS. Rotterdam, Museum Boymans

94 (Cat. No. 89) STUDIES OF ARMS AND A MAN'S FACE. London, Victoria and Albert Museum

95 (Cat. No. 85) STUDY FOR DANIEL IN THE LIONS' DEN. New York, Pierpont Morgan Library

96 (Cat. No. 83) A LIONESS. London, British Museum

97 (Cat. No. 86) THE REVEREND HENDRIK VAN THULDEN. London, British Museum

98 (Cat. No. 84) A MAN STANDING. Munich, Graphische Sammlungen

99 (Cat. No. 90) YOUNG WOMAN CROUCHING. Vienna, Albertina

100 (Cat. No. 98) PORTRAIT OF A LITTLE BOY. Vienna, Albertina

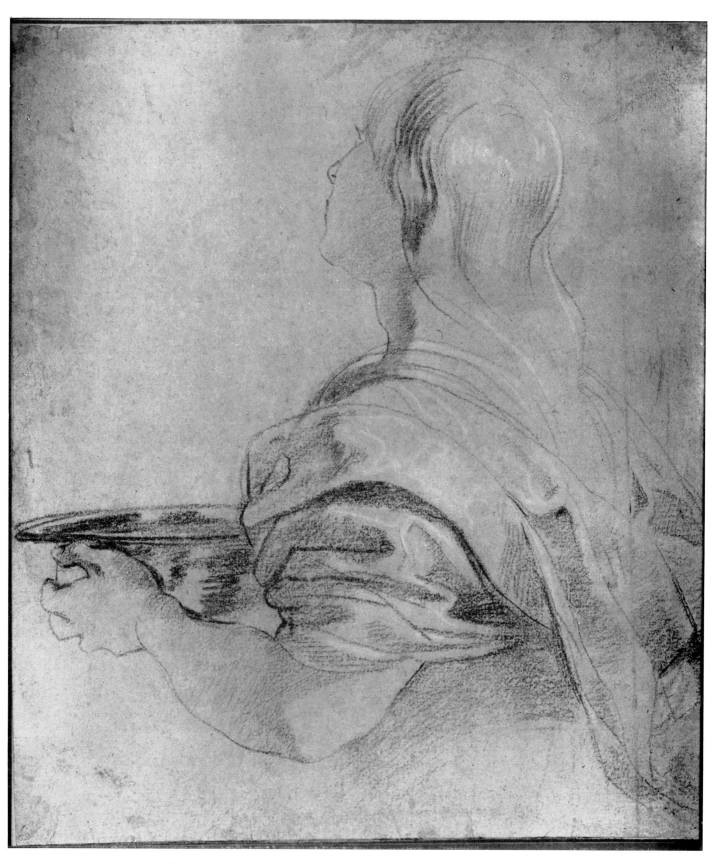

101 (Cat. No. 94) YOUNG WOMAN HOLDING A BOWL. Vienna, Albertina

102 (Cat. No. 99) YOUNG MAN CARRYING A LADDER. Vienna, Albertina

103 (Cat. No. 95) PEASANT GIRL CHURNING BUTTER. Chatsworth, Devonshire Collection

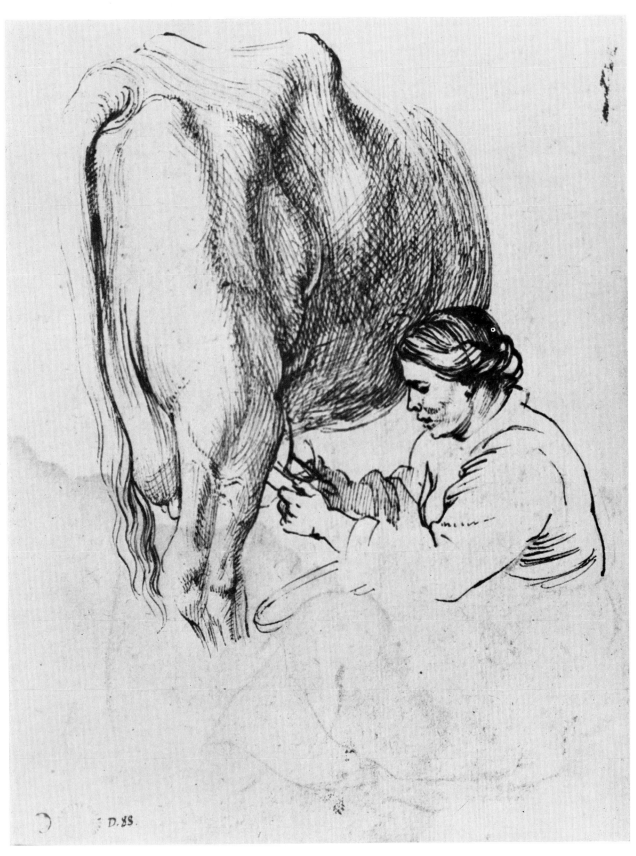

104 (Cat. No. 88) WOMAN MILKING A COW. Besançon, Musée des Beaux-Arts

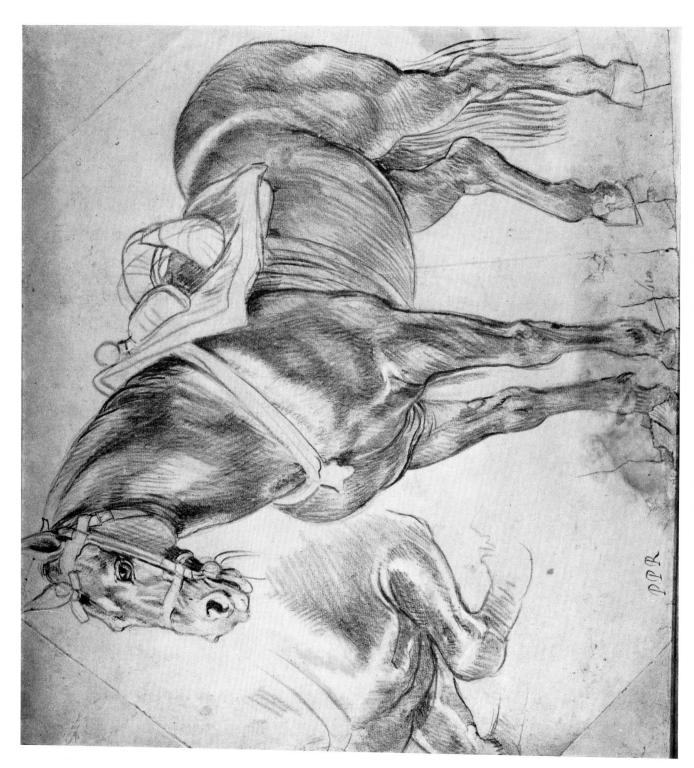

105 (Cat. No. 87) A SADDLED HORSE. Vienna, Albertina

106 (Cat. No. 91) A BULLOCK. Vienna, Albertina

107 (Cat. No. 92) STUDY FOR ST. FRANCIS. Paris, Collection of Frits Lugt

108 (Cat. No. 93) TWO FRANCISCAN MONKS. Chatsworth, Devonshire Collection

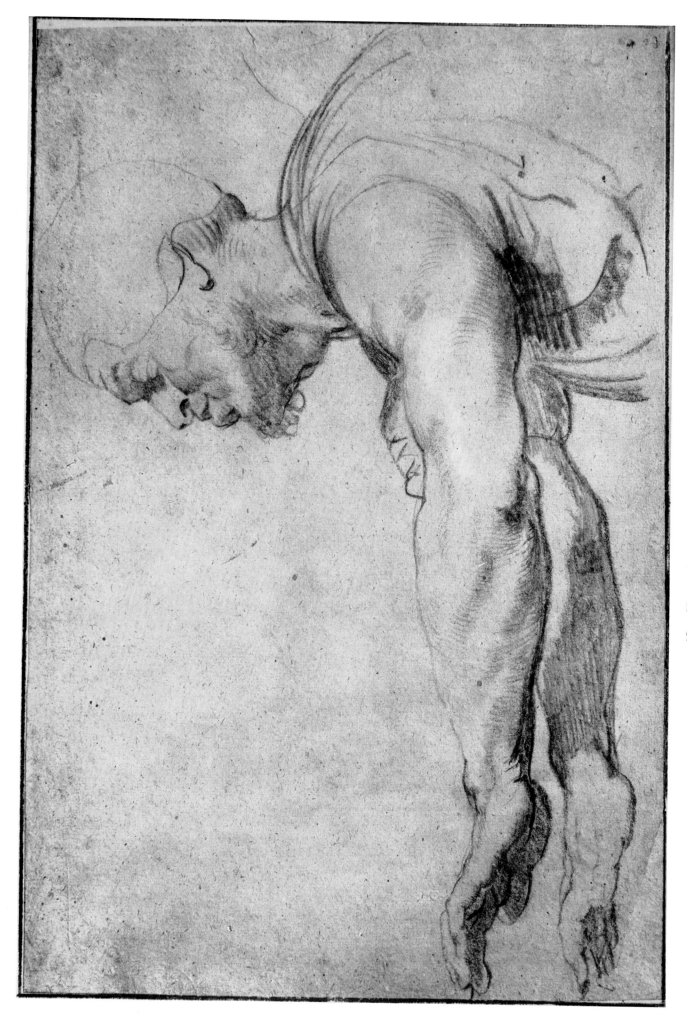

109 (Cat. No. 100) A BLIND MAN. Vienna, Albertina

110 (Cat. No. 96) A MAN THRUSTING WITH A LANCE. Glasgow, Collection of Sir Archibald Campbell

111 (Cat. No. 97) A MAN FALLING FROM A HORSE. London, British Museum

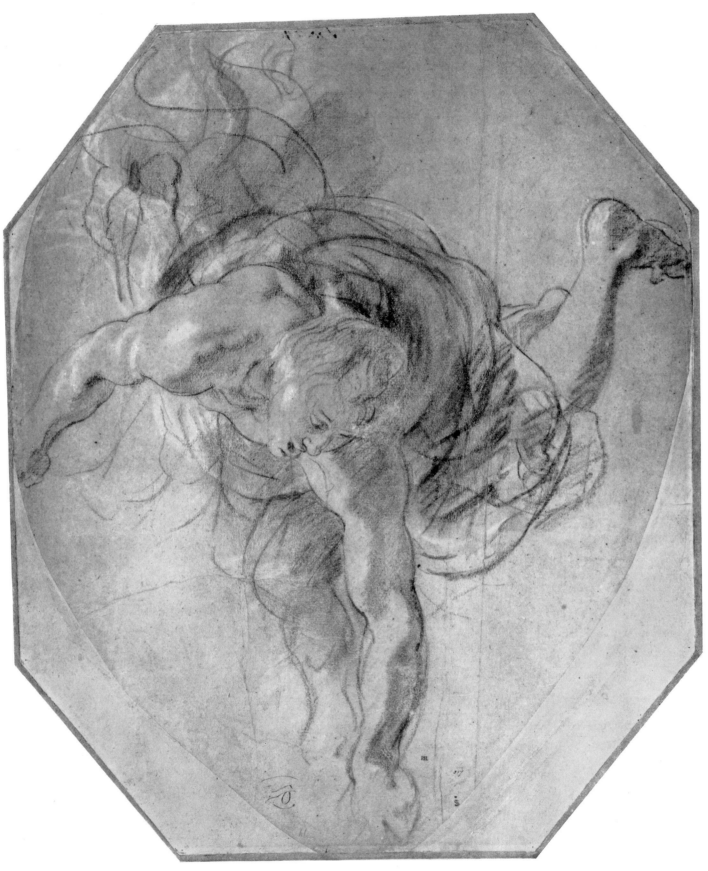

112 (Cat. No. 102) A STUDY FOR MERCURY DESCENDING. London, Victoria and Albert Museum

113 (Cat. No. 101) ROBIN, THE DWARF OF THE EARL OF ARUNDEL. Stockholm, Nationalmuseum

114 (Cat. No. 104) PORTRAIT OF SUSANNE FOURMENT. Rotterdam, Museum Boymans

115 (Cat. No. 103) PORTRAIT OF ISABELLA BRANT. London, British Museum

116 (Cat. No. 106) PORTRAIT OF A YOUNG GIRL. Vienna, Albertina

117 (Cat. No. 108) PORTRAIT OF RUBENS' SON NICOLAS. Vienna, Albertina

118 (Cat. No. 109) PORTRAIT OF RUBENS' SON NICOLAS. Vienna, Albertina

119 (Cat. No. 107) PORTRAIT OF GEORGE VILLIERS, DUKE OF BUCKINGHAM. Vienna, Albertina

120 (Cat. No. 112) PORTRAIT OF A YOUNG GIRL. Leningrad, Hermitage

121 (Cat. No. 110) YOUNG WOMAN WITH CROSSED HANDS. Rotterdam, Museum Boymans

122 (Cat. No. 113) YOUNG WOMAN LOOKING DOWN. Florence, Uffizi

123 (Cat. No. 105) JESUIT MISSIONARY IN CHINESE COSTUME. New York, Pierpont Morgan Library

124 (Cat. No. 111) PORTRAIT OF KING PHILIP IV OF SPAIN. Bayonne, Musée Bonnat

125 (Cat. No. 114) PORTRAIT OF HÉLÈNE FOURMENT. London, Collection of Count Antoine Seilern

126 (Cat. No. 123) SELF-PORTRAIT. Paris, Louvre

127 (Cat. No. 116) YOUNG WOMAN HOLDING A TRAY. Paris, Collection of Frits Lugt

128 (Cat. No. 117) A PEASANT WOMAN, WALKING. Florence, Uffizi

129 (Cat. No. 115) PORTRAIT OF HÉLÈNE FOURMENT. Rotterdam, Museum Boymans

130 (Cat. No. 118) YOUNG WOMAN WITH OSTRICH FAN. Paris, Louvre

131 (Cat. No. 120) A YOUNG COUPLE. Amsterdam, Fodor Collection

132 (Cat. No. 121) A YOUNG WOMAN, KNEELING. Amsterdam, Fodor Collection

133 (Cat. No. 124) YOUNG WOMAN WITH RAISED ARMS. Paris, Louvre

134 (Cat. No. 119) A YOUNG MAN, WALKING. Amsterdam, Fodor Collection

135 (Cat. No. 125) HEAD AND FEET OF A CHILD. Besançon, Musée des Beaux-Arts

136 (Cat. No. 122) HEAD OF ST. FRANCIS.
Frankfurt, Städelsches Kunstinstitut

137 (Cat. No. 127) PORTRAIT OF FRANS RUBENS. Rotterdam, Museum Boymans

138 (Cat. No. 128) A SMALL CHILD. Paris, Louvre

139 (Cat. No. 126) SELF-PORTRAIT. Windsor Castle, Royal Library

III
LANDSCAPES

140 (Cat. No. 131) LANDSCAPE WITH FALLEN TREE. Paris, Louvre

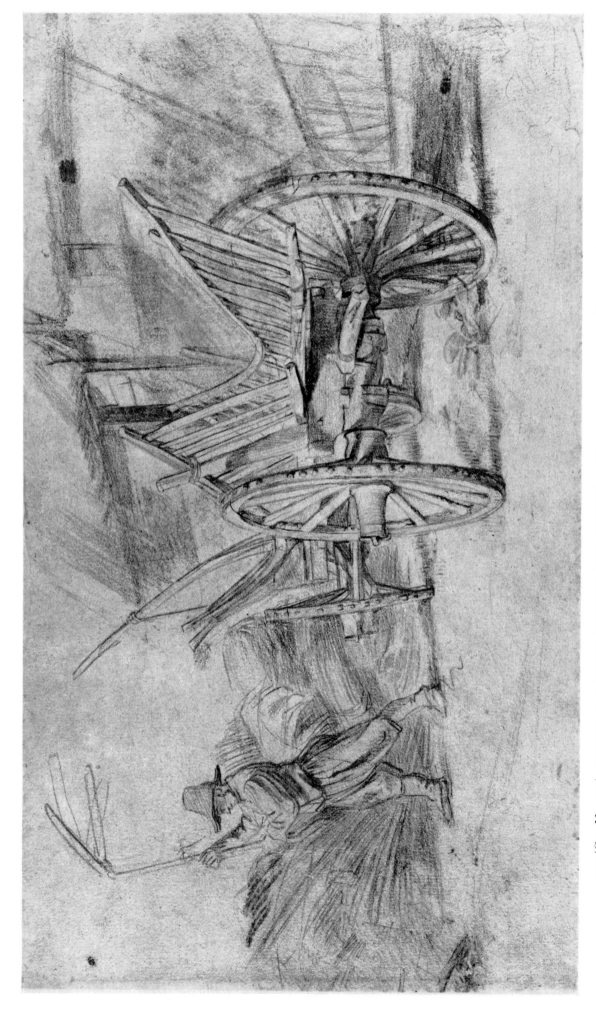

141 (Cat. No. 129) FARMYARD WITH FARMER THRESHING, AND A HAY-WAGON. Chatsworth, Devonshire Collection

142 (Cat. No. 133) TWO FARM WAGONS. Berlin, Kupferstichkabinett

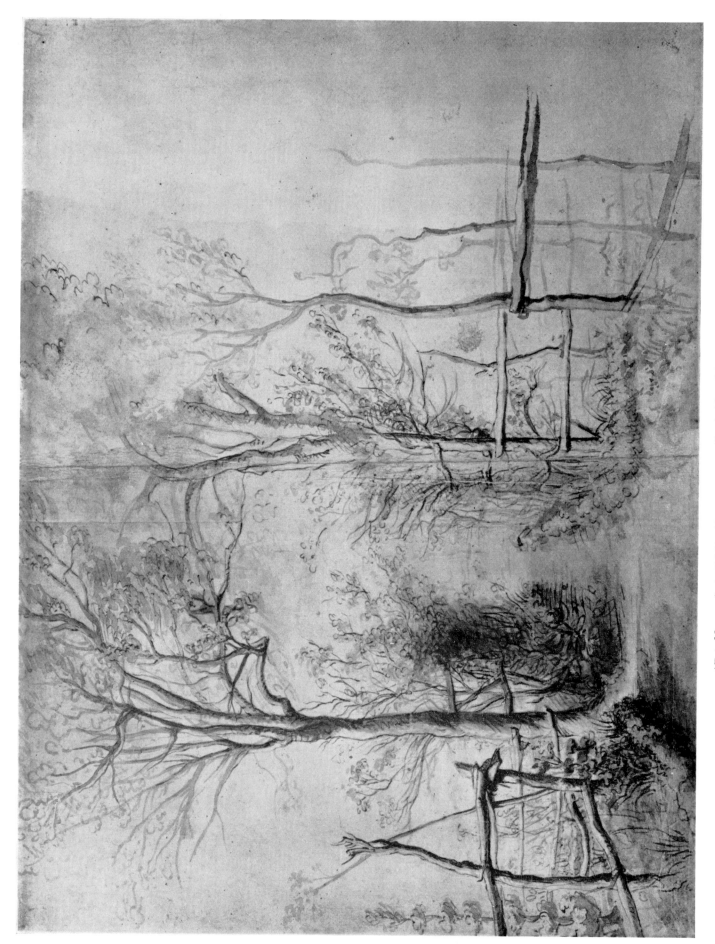

143 (Cat. No. 130) A COUNTRY LANE. Cambridge, Fitzwilliam Museum

144 (Cat. No. 132) A FALLEN TREE. Chatsworth, Devonshire Collection

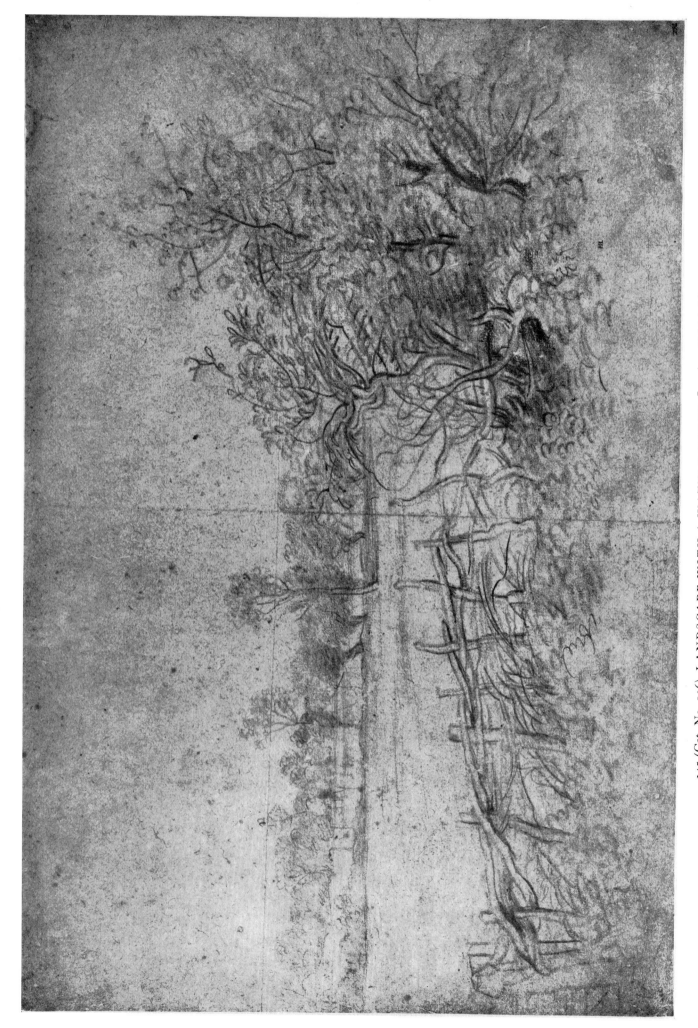

145 (Cat. No. 136) LANDSCAPE WITH A WATTLE FENCE. London, British Museum

146 (Cat. No. 137) WOODLAND SCENE. Oxford, Ashmolean Museum

147 (Cat. No. 134) A WILLOW TREE. London, British Museum

IV
DESIGNS FOR SCULPTURES, ENGRAVINGS AND WOODCUTS

148 (Cat. No. 138) VIRTUE AND HONOUR. Antwerp, Musée Plantin

149 (Cat. No. 144) AN ANGEL BLOWING A TRUMPET. New York, Pierpont Morgan Library

150 (Cat. No. 145) AN ANGEL BLOWING A TRUMPET. New York, Pierpont Morgan Library

151 (Cat. No. 139) THE ADORATION OF THE MAGI. New York, Pierpont Morgan Library

152 (Cat. No. 141) PORTRAIT OF JUSTUS LIPSIUS. London, British Museum

153 (Cat. No. 142) THE HOLY FAMILY AND ST. JOHN. London, British Museum

154 (Cat. No. 143) THE ADORATION OF THE SHEPHERDS. Paris, Collection of Frits Lugt

155 (Cat. No. 140) DESIGN FOR THE TITLE-PAGE OF THE BREVIARIUM ROMANUM.
London, British Museum

156 (Cat. No. 146) DESIGN FOR THE TITLE-PAGE OF FRANCISCUS HARAEUS' ANNALES
DUCUM BRABANTIAE. London, British Museum

157 (Cat. No. 147) THE ANNUNCIATION. Vienna, Albertina

158 (Cat. No. 151) TITLE-PAGE FOR THE WORKS OF LUDOVICUS BLOSIUS. London, British Museum

159 (Cat. No. 153) POETRY AND VIRTUE. Antwerp, Musée Plantin

160 (Cat. No. 148) THE EMBLEM OF THE PLANTIN PRESS. Antwerp, Musée Plantin

161 (Cat. No. 154) SAMSON AND THE LION. Antwerp, Musée Plantin

162 (Cat. No. 152) THE GARDEN OF LOVE. New York, Metropolitan Museum of Art

163 (Cat. No. 152) THE GARDEN OF LOVE. New York, Metropolitan Museum of Art

164 (Cat. No. 155) MARCH OF SILENUS. Paris, Louvre

V

COPIES BY RUBENS AFTER OTHER MASTERS AND DRAWINGS RETOUCHED BY RUBENS

165 (Cat. No. 162) ELEVEN HEADS OF WOMEN. Brunswick, Herzog Anton Ulrich-Museum

166 (Cat. No. 156) TWO COPIES AFTER TOBIAS
STIMMER. London, Private Collection

167 (Cat. No. 157) A YOUNG COUPLE, AFTER
VAN MECKENEM. Berlin, Kupferstichkabinett

168 (Cat. No. 159) *THE FLIGHT OF MEDEA*. Rotterdam, Museum Boymans

169 (Cat. No. 160) *THREE FIGURES FROM A ROMAN SARCOPHAGUS*. Chicago, Art Institute

170 (Cat. No. 165) THE HEAD OF SENECA. Leningrad, Hermitage

171 (Cat. No. 158) IGNUDO, AFTER MICHELANGELO. London, British Museum

172 (Cat. No. 166) THREE CARYATIDS, AFTER PRIMATICCIO. Rotterdam, Museum Boymans

173 (Cat. No. 161) THE FIGHT FOR THE STANDARD, AFTER LEONARDO DA VINCI. Paris, Louvre

174 (Cat. No. 167) ECCE HOMO, AFTER TITIAN. London, Collection of Victor Koch

175 (Cat. No. 163) FIGURES IN ORIENTAL DRESS. London, British Museum

176 (Cat. No. 163) FIGURES IN ORIENTAL DRESS. London, British Museum

177 (Cat. No. 170) GOD THE FATHER. London, Victoria and Albert Museum

178 (Cat. No. 168) YOUNG WOMAN HOLDING A SHIELD. Chatsworth, Devonshire Collection

179 (Cat. No. 164) HEAD OF SILENUS. New York, Metropolitan Museum

LIST OF PLATES

LIST OF PLATES

SKETCHES FOR COMPOSITIONS

1. (Cat. No. 1). *The Discovery of Callisto*. Berlin, Kupferstichkabinett
2. (Cat. No. 2). *A Battle of Greeks and Amazons*. London, British Museum
3. (Cat. No. 5). *Christ Crowned with Thorns*. Brunswick, Herzog Anton Ulrich-Museum
4. (Cat. No. 3). *The Descent from the Cross*. Leningrad, Hermitage.
5. (Cat. No. 4). *The Entombment of Christ*. Rotterdam, Museum Boymans
6. (Cat. No. 6). *The Return of the Victorious Horatius*. New York, Metropolitan Museum of Art
7. (Cat. No. 7). *Sketches for the Last Supper*. Chatsworth, Devonshire Collection
8. (Cat. No. 7 verso). *Medea and Her Slain Children*. Reverse of Plate 7. Chatsworth, Devonshire Collection
9. (Cat. No. 8). *Studies for the Suicide of Thisbe*. Paris, Louvre
10. (Cat. No. 9). *Thisbe Committing Suicide*. Brunswick (Maine), Collection of Mrs. Stanley P. Chase
11. (Cat. No. 12). *The Birth of the Virgin*. Paris, Petit Palais
12. (Cat. No. 11). *The Baptism of Christ*. Paris, Louvre
13. (Cat. No. 13). *The Death of Creusa*. Bayonne, Musée Bonnat
14. (Cat. No. 14). *The Battle of Lapiths and Centaurs*. Amsterdam, Rijksmuseum
15. (Cat. No. 10). *Cain Slaying Abel*. Amsterdam, Fodor Collection
16. (Cat. No. 15). *Judith Killing Holofernes*. Frankfurt, Städelsches Kunstinstitut
17. (Cat. No. 20). *Susanna*. Montpellier, Bibliothèque Universitaire
18. (Cat. No. 16). *St. Gregory, St. Maurus and St. Papianus*. Chantilly, Musée Condé
19. (Cat. No. 17). *The Image of the Virgin Adored by Angels*. Vienna, Albertina
20. (Cat. No. 18). *Two Shepherds and Man with Turban*. Amsterdam, Fodor Collection
21. (Cat. No. 24). *Samson and Delila*. Amsterdam, Collection of J. Q. van Regteren Altena
22. (Cat. No. 23). *Venus Lamenting Adonis*. London, Collection of Ludwig Burchard
23. (Cat. No. 22). *Venus Lamenting Adonis*. London, British Museum
24. (Cat. No. 21). *The Death of Hippolytus*. Bayonne, Musée Bonnat
25. (Cat. No. 19). *A Bacchanal*. Antwerp, Cabinet des Estampes
26. (Cat. No. 30). *Two Studies for St. Christopher*. London, British Museum
27. (Cat. No. 25). *David and Goliath*. Rotterdam, Museum Boymans
28. (Cat. No. 26). *David and Goliath*. Montpellier, Bibliothèque Universitaire
29. (Cat. No. 31). *The Conversion of St. Paul*. London, Collection of Count Antoine Seilern
30. (Cat. No. 29). *Silenus and Aegle, and Other Figures*. Windsor Castle, Royal Library
31. (Cat. No. 32). *Bathsheba Receiving David's Letter*. Berlin, Kupferstichkabinett
32. (Cat. No. 34). *Hercules Strangling the Nemean Lion*. Antwerp, Cabinet des Estampes

33. (Cat. No. 27). *Studies for the Visitation*. Bayonne, Musée Bonnat
34. (Cat. No. 28). *Studies for the Presentation in the Temple*. New York, Metropolitan Museum of Art
35. (Cat. No. 37). *The Entombment of Christ*. Amsterdam, Rijksmuseum
36. (Cat. No. 33). *Two Studies of a River-God*. Boston, Museum of Fine Arts
37. (Cat. No. 36). *Three Robed Men*. Copenhagen, Kunstmuseet
38. (Cat. No. 35). *The Assumption of the Virgin*. Vienna, Albertina
39. (Cat. No. 42). *The Descent from the Cross*. Collection of the late Mrs. G. W. Wrangham
40. (Cat. No. 38). *The Continence of Scipio*. Berlin, Kupferstichkabinett
41. (Cat. No. 39). *The Continence of Scipio*. Bayonne, Musée Bonnat
42. (Cat. No. 41). *Studies for a Drunken Silenus*. Collection of the late Mrs. G. W. Wrangham
43. (Cat. No. 43). *The Raising of Lazarus*. Berlin, Kupferstichkabinett
44. (Cat. No. 40). *The Apostles Surrounding the Virgin's Tomb*. Oslo, Nasjionalgalleriet
45. (Cat. No. 44). *The Last Communion of St. Francis*. Antwerp, Cabinet des Estampes
46. (Cat. No. 45). *Female Nudes Reclining*. London, Collection of Count Antoine Seilern
47. (Cat. No. 46). *Studies for Venus and Cupid*. New York, Frick Collection
48. (Cat. No. 48). *Hercules Standing on Discord, Crowned by Two Genii*. London, British Museum
49. (Cat. No. 47). *St. Gregory Nazianzenus*. New York, Collection of Clarence L. Hay
50. (Cat. No. 52). *Studies for a Roman Triumph*. Berlin, Kupferstichkabinett
51. (Cat. No. 49). *Roma Triumphans*. Vienna, Albertina
52. (Cat. No. 50 recto). *The Vestal Tuccia*. Paris, Louvre
53. (Cat. No. 50 verso). *Louis XIII Comes of Age*. Paris, Louvre
54. (Cat. No. 51 recto). *Marie de Médicis Receives the Olive Branch of Peace*. Formerly Bremen, Kunsthalle
55. (Cat. No. 51 verso). *Henry IV Carried to Heaven and Other Figures*. Reverse of Plate 54. Formerly Bremen, Kunsthalle
56. (Cat. No. 55). *Female Nudes Reclining*. London, Collection of Count Antoine Seilern
57. (Cat. No. 55 verso). *Centaurs Embracing*. Reverse of Plate 56
58. (Cat. No. 53 verso). *Studies for the Virgin and Child and Studies for St. George and the Dragon*. Reverse of Plate 59
59. (Cat. No. 53 recto). *The Virgin Adored by Saints*. Stockholm, Nationalmuseum
60. (Cat. No. 53 verso). *St. George and the Dragon*. Detail of Plate 58
61. (Cat. No. 54). *Studies for St. George and the Princess*. Berlin, Kupferstichkabinett
62. (Cat. No. 58). *Venus Anadyomene and Two Nereids*. London, British Museum
63. (Cat. No. 56). *A Nymph Asleep*. Rotterdam, Museum Boymans
64. (Cat. No. 62). *The Three Graces*. London, Collection of Count Antoine Seilern

LANDSCAPES

DESIGNS FOR SCULPTURES, ENGRAVINGS AND WOODCUTS

COPIES BY RUBENS AFTER OTHER MASTERS AND DRAWINGS RETOUCHED BY RUBENS

LIST OF COLLECTIONS

ACKNOWLEDGEMENT

The Author and Publishers wish to express their gratitude to the Directors of Museums and Public Collections, as well as to all Private Collectors who kindly provided photographs and gave permission for reproduction